First World War
and Army of Occupation
War Diary
France, Belgium and Germany

62 DIVISION
Divisional Troops
Divisional Trench Mortar Batteries
1 February 1917 - 31 March 1919

WO95/3075/4

The Naval & Military Press Ltd
www.nmarchive.com
Published in association with The National Archives

Published by

The Naval & Military Press Ltd

Unit 10 Ridgewood Industrial Park,
Uckfield, East Sussex,
TN22 5QE England
Tel: +44 (0) 1825 749494

www.naval-military-press.com

www.nmarchive.com

This diary has been reprinted in facsimile from the original. Any imperfections are inevitably reproduced and the quality may fall short of modern type and cartographic standards.

© **Crown Copyright**
Images reproduced by permission of The National Archives, London, England, 2015.

Contents

Document type	Place/Title	Date From	Date To
Heading	WO95/3075 (4)		
Heading	62nd Trench Mortar Bty Feb 1917 1919 Mar		
Heading	War Diary 62nd Division Trench Mortar Batteries Volume I From July 1st 1917 July 28.1917		
War Diary	Valheureux.	01/02/1917	06/02/1917
War Diary	Bertrancourt.	07/02/1917	27/02/1917
War Diary	Engelsart.	28/02/1917	28/02/1917
Heading	War Diary 62nd Division Trench Mortar Batteries		
War Diary	Mailly	01/03/1917	07/03/1917
War Diary	Engelsart.	08/03/1917	08/03/1917
War Diary	Mailly	08/03/1917	20/03/1917
War Diary	Mailly Maillet	21/03/1917	21/03/1917
War Diary	Miraumont	22/03/1917	31/03/1917
Heading	War Diary Trench Mortar Batteries 62nd Division Volume III From April 1st 17 To April 30th 17		
War Diary	Miruamont	01/04/1917	01/04/1917
War Diary	Achiet Le Grand	02/04/1917	29/04/1917
Heading	62 Div May (1) 1917		
Heading	War Diary 62nd Division Trench Mortar Batteries Volume IV. From May 1st 1917 to May 31st 1917		
War Diary		01/05/1917	31/05/1917
Heading	62 Div June 1917		
Heading	War Diary Trench Mortar Batteries 62nd Division Volume 1 From 1st June 1917 To 30th June 1917		
War Diary	Sapignies	01/06/1917	23/06/1917
War Diary	Beugnatre	24/06/1917	30/06/1917
Heading	War Diary of Divisional Trench Mortar Batteries Volume VI From 1st July 1917 To 31st July 1917		
War Diary	Behagnies	01/07/1917	04/07/1917
War Diary	Vaulx	05/07/1917	31/07/1917
Heading	War Diary of 62nd Divisional Trench Mortar Batteries Volume VII From 1st August 1917 To 31st August 1917		
War Diary	Vaulx	01/08/1917	04/08/1917
War Diary	Bullecourt	08/08/1917	10/08/1917
War Diary	Noreuil	11/08/1917	12/08/1917
War Diary	Bullecourt	13/08/1917	14/08/1917
War Diary	Noreuil	15/08/1917	16/08/1917
War Diary	Vaulx	16/08/1917	16/08/1917
War Diary	Noreuil	17/08/1917	17/08/1917
War Diary	Bullecourt	17/08/1917	17/08/1917
War Diary	Noreuil	18/08/1917	18/08/1917
War Diary	Bullecourt	18/08/1917	18/08/1917
War Diary	Noreuil	18/08/1917	18/08/1917
War Diary	Bullecourt	19/08/1917	19/08/1917
War Diary	Noreuil	20/08/1917	20/08/1917
War Diary	Bullecourt	20/08/1917	20/08/1917
War Diary	Noreuil	21/08/1917	21/08/1917
War Diary	Bullecourt	21/08/1917	21/08/1917
War Diary	Noreuil	22/08/1917	22/08/1917

War Diary	Bullecourt	22/08/1917	23/08/1917
War Diary	Noreuil	23/08/1917	23/08/1917
War Diary	Bullecourt	24/08/1917	25/08/1917
War Diary	Noreuil	26/08/1917	31/08/1917
Miscellaneous	Reference BMF/1892/9		
Heading	War Diary Of 62nd Divisional Trench Mortar Batteries Volume VIII From 1st September 1917 to 30th September 1917		
War Diary	Noreuil	01/09/1917	04/09/1917
War Diary	Bullecourt	04/09/1917	05/09/1917
War Diary	Noreuil	06/09/1917	07/09/1917
War Diary	Bullecourt	07/09/1917	07/09/1917
War Diary	Noreuil	08/09/1917	08/09/1917
War Diary	Bullecourt	08/09/1917	08/09/1917
War Diary	Noreuil	09/09/1917	09/09/1917
War Diary	Bullecourt	09/09/1917	09/09/1917
War Diary	Noreuil	10/09/1917	10/09/1917
War Diary	Bullecourt	10/09/1917	10/09/1917
War Diary	Vaulx	10/09/1917	10/09/1917
War Diary	Noreuil	11/09/1917	11/09/1917
War Diary	Bullecourt	11/09/1917	11/09/1917
War Diary	Noreuil	12/09/1917	12/09/1917
War Diary	Bullecourt	12/09/1917	12/09/1917
War Diary	Noreuil	13/09/1917	13/09/1917
War Diary	Vaulx	14/09/1917	14/09/1917
War Diary	Noreuil	15/09/1917	18/09/1917
War Diary	Vaulx	18/09/1917	18/09/1917
War Diary	Noreuil	19/09/1917	27/09/1917
War Diary	Bullecourt	27/09/1917	28/09/1917
War Diary	Vaulx	28/09/1917	28/09/1917
War Diary	Bullecourt	29/09/1917	30/09/1917
Heading	62 Div October 1917		
Heading	War Diary of 62nd Divisional Trench Mortar Batteries Volume IX From 1st October 1917 To 31st October 1917		
War Diary	Vaulx	01/10/1917	01/10/1917
War Diary	Noreuil	02/10/1917	04/10/1917
War Diary	Bullecourt	04/10/1917	04/10/1917
War Diary	Noreuil	05/10/1917	07/10/1917
War Diary	Bullecourt	07/10/1917	09/10/1917
War Diary	Noreuil	10/10/1917	10/10/1917
War Diary	Bullecourt	11/10/1917	12/10/1917
War Diary	Noreuil	13/10/1917	17/10/1917
War Diary	Bullecourt	17/10/1917	17/10/1917
War Diary	Noreuil	18/10/1917	18/10/1917
War Diary	Vaulx	19/10/1917	19/10/1917
War Diary	Bapaume	20/10/1917	31/10/1917
War Diary	War Diary Of Divisional Trench Mortar Batteries Volume X From 1st November 1917 to 30th November 1917		
War Diary	Bapaume	01/11/1917	09/11/1917
War Diary	Rauyalcourt	10/11/1917	30/11/1917
Heading	62nd F.M.B. December 1917		
War Diary	Rayaulcourt	01/12/1917	28/12/1917
War Diary	Cauchin Legal	23/12/1917	31/12/1917

Heading	War Diary of 62nd Division Trench Mortar Batteries Volume VIII From 1st January 1918. To 31st January 1918. Vol 12		
War Diary	Gauchin Cejal	01/01/1918	02/01/1918
War Diary	Combly Neul	03/01/1918	07/01/1918
War Diary	Roclincourt	08/01/1918	31/01/1918
Heading	War Diary of 62nd Divisional Trench Mortar Batteries. Volume 13 From February 1st 1916 To February 28th 1918.		
War Diary	Roclincourt	01/02/1918	28/02/1918
Heading	D.T.M.O. 62nd Division March 1918		
Heading	War Diary Trench Mortar Batteries. 62nd Division. Volume 3. From March 1st 18. To March 31st 18.		
War Diary	Cambligneul.	01/03/1918	07/03/1918
War Diary	Roclincourt.	08/03/1918	24/03/1918
War Diary	Berles	25/03/1918	31/03/1918
Heading	Divisional Trench Mortar Officer 62nd Division April 1918		
Heading	Trench Mortar Batteries 62nd Division From April 1st 18 To April 30th 18		
War Diary	Souastre	01/04/1918	02/04/1918
War Diary	Gommecourt	05/04/1918	10/04/1918
War Diary	Souastre.	11/04/1918	11/04/1918
War Diary	Monchy Au Bois	12/04/1918	26/04/1918
War Diary	Authie.	27/04/1918	27/04/1918
Heading	War Diary Trench Mortar Batteries 62nd Division Volume 17		
War Diary	Authie.	01/05/1918	20/05/1918
War Diary	Couin	21/05/1918	02/06/1918
Heading	War Diary 62nd Divisional Trench Mortar 62nd Division Volume 6 From June 1st 1918 To June 30th 1918		
War Diary	Couin	01/06/1918	25/06/1918
War Diary	Orville.	26/06/1918	30/06/1918
Heading	62nd Division Trench Mortar Batteries July 1918		
Heading	War Diary Trench Mortar Batteries 62nd Division From July 1st 1918 To July 31st 1918 Volume 7		
War Diary	Orville	01/07/1918	15/07/1918
War Diary	Arcis	16/07/1918	19/07/1918
War Diary	Mutigny	20/07/1918	20/07/1918
War Diary	Germaine	20/07/1918	30/07/1918
Heading	War Diary Of Divisional Ammunition Column Volume XX From 1st August 1918 To 31st August 1918		
War Diary	Ref Map Chalons	01/08/1918	02/08/1918
War Diary	57	03/08/1918	10/08/1918
War Diary	Ref Map 57d 1/40,0000	11/08/1918	28/08/1918
War Diary	54. C 1/40,000	29/08/1918	29/08/1918
War Diary	Ref Map 57c 1/40,000	30/08/1918	31/08/1918
Heading	War Diary Trench Mortar Batteries 62nd Division. Volume XXI From Sept 1st 1918 To Sept 30th 1918		
War Diary	Gomiecourt.	01/09/1918	08/09/1918
War Diary	Beugny	09/09/1918	28/09/1918
War Diary	Royalcourt	29/09/1918	30/09/1918
War Diary	War Diary Trench Mortar Bties 62nd Division Volume 22 From 1st 1918 To Oct 31st 1918		
War Diary	Havrincourt	01/10/1918	12/10/1918

War Diary	Masieres	13/10/1918	14/10/1918
War Diary	Crevecoeur	15/10/1918	17/10/1918
War Diary	Beruvois	18/10/1918	20/10/1918
War Diary	Quary	21/10/1918	25/10/1918
War Diary	St Python	26/10/1918	31/10/1918
Heading	War Diary 62nd Trench Mortar Bties 62nd Division Volume 11 From Nov 1st 18 To Nov 30th 18		
War Diary	St Python	01/11/1918	04/11/1918
War Diary	Escarmrin	05/11/1918	06/11/1918
War Diary	Fragmoy	07/11/1918	08/11/1918
War Diary	Lecarnoy	09/11/1918	09/11/1918
War Diary	Narcnies	10/11/1918	11/11/1918
War Diary	Neuf Mesnil	15/11/1918	17/11/1918
War Diary	Srus Le Bois	18/11/1918	19/11/1918
War Diary	St Python	20/11/1918	30/11/1918
Heading	War Diary Trench Mortar Bties 62nd Division Volume 12 From Dec 1st 18 to Dec 31st 18		
War Diary	St Pyton	01/12/1918	02/12/1918
War Diary	Cambrai	02/12/1918	23/12/1918
War Diary	Euskirchen	20/12/1918	27/12/1918
War Diary	Olef	28/12/1918	31/12/1918
War Diary	Olef	01/01/1919	04/02/1919
War Diary	Urft.	05/02/1919	28/02/1919
Heading	War Diary Trench Mortar Batteries Highland Division Volume B 27 From March 1st 1919. To March 31st 1919		
War Diary	Urft.	01/03/1919	31/03/1919

WO 95/30275 (4)

62ND DIVISION

62ND TRENCH MORTAR BTY
FEB 1917 ~~DEC 1918~~
1919 MAR

Original.

War Diary.

62nd. Divisional Trench.

Mortar Batteries.

Volume I

From. Feby 1st. 1917.
To. Feby 28. 1917.

Original.

Army Form C. 2118.
T.M.B.1.

WAR DIARY
or
INTELLIGENCE SUMMARY.
(Erase heading not required)

62nd Divisional Trench Mortar Batteries

Instructions regarding War Diaries and Intelligence Summaries are contained in F.S. Regs., Part II. and the Staff Manual respectively. Title pages will be prepared in manuscript.

Place	Date	Hour	Summary of Events and Information	Remarks and references to Appendices
VALHEUREUX.	1/2/17.		All personnel of the Trench Mortar Batteries 62nd Division, attending the fourth course at the Fifth Army Trench Mortar School.	
do	2/2/17		Nothing to report.	
do	3/2/17		do	
do	4/2/17		do	
do	5/2/17		do	
do	6/2/17		Personnel of the Trench Mortar Batteries proceeded from the Fifth Army Trench Mortar School and were attached to 62nd Divisional Ammunition Column at BERTRANCOURT.	
BERTRANCOURT.	7/2/17 to 17/2/17		Nothing to report.	
BERTRANCOURT.	18/2/17		Batteries proceeded to MAILLY- MAILLET and took over Billet 120 from the Trench Mortar Batteries 32nd Division.	
do	19/2/17 to 27/2/17		Nothing to report.	
ENGELBERT.	28/2/17	4a.m.	Two Medium Trench Mortars of Z/62 Trench Mortar Battery were taken up to Infantry Brigade Head Quarters to be in readiness to fire on GOODS TRENCHES if required.	

Lieut R.F.A.
D.T.M.O. 62nd Division.

Original

Vol II

War Diary

62nd Divisional Trench

Mortar Batteries

Volumne II

From 1st March 1917

To 31st March 1917.

Army Form C. 2118.

WAR DIARY
or
INTELLIGENCE SUMMARY.

Trench Mortar Batteries.
62nd Division.

(Erase heading not required.)

Place	Date	Hour	Summary of Events and Information	Remarks and references to Appendices
Mailly.	1/3/17		Nothing to report.	
do	2/3/17		do	
Mailly.	3/3/17		2 Officers and 40 Other Ranks proceeded to HAMEL for work on Ammunition Dump.	
do	4/3/17 to 7/3/17		Nothing to report.	
Engelbart.	8/3/17		Two Medium Trench Mortars of Z/62 brought back from MIRAUMONT.	
Mailly.	do		V/62 Heavy Trench Mortar Battery transfered to THIRD ARMY. Proceeded by road to 7th Corps Seige Park.	
do	do		Eleven Medium Mortars in possession handed over to 7th Division D.T.M.O., who entrained at ACHEUX proceeding to FIRST ARMY.	
do	8/3/17 to 20/3/17		Nothing to report.	
Mailly - Mallet.	21/3/17		Personnel of Trench Mortar Batteries proceeded to MIRAUMONT and attached to 62nd D.A.C. for work on Ammunition Dump.	
Miraumont.	22/3/17 to 31/3/17		Nothing to report.	

Lieut. R.F.A.
D.T.M.O. 62nd Div Artillery.

Instructions regarding War Diaries and Intelligence Summaries are contained in F. S. Regs., Part II. and the Staff Manual respectively. Title pages will be prepared in manuscript.

Original.

War Diary.

Trench Mortar Batteries.

62nd. Division.

Volume III

From April 1st. 17.
To. April 30rd. 17.

Vol 3

Army Form C. 2118.

WAR DIARY
~~INTELLIGENCE~~ SUMMARY

Trench Mortar Batteries.
62nd Division.

(Erase heading not required.)

Instructions regarding War Diaries and Intelligence Summaries are contained in F. S. Regs., Part II. and the Staff Manual respectively. Title pages will be prepared in manuscript.

Place	Date	Hour	Summary of Events and Information	Remarks and references to Appendices
MIRAUMONT	1-4-17.		Personnel of X.Y.and Z. Batteries proceeded to ACHIET LE GRAND.	
ACHIET LE GRAND.	2-4-17 to 28-4-17		Nothing to report.	
ACHIET LE GRAND.	29-4-17.		Personnel of V/62 Trench Mortar Battery returned from 51st Div Arty.	
ditt.	30-4-17.		Nothing to report.	
	30-4-17.			

[signature] Lieut R.F.A.
D.T.M.O. 62nd Div Arty.

62 DIV

May (1)
1917

Original.

Vol 4

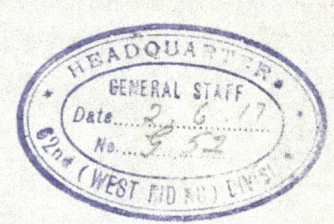

War Diary

62nd. Divisional

Trench Mortar Batteries.

Volume IV.

From   May 1st. 1917
To   May 31st. 1917.

Army Form C. 2118.

WAR DIARY

~~INTELLIGENCE~~ SUMMARY

Trench Mortar Batteries,
62nd. Division.

(Erase heading not required.)

		Summary of Events and Information	Remarks and references to Appendices
	11-5-17 to 12-5-17	Nothing to report.	
ditto	13-5-17	Personnel of V/62 T.M.Batteries proceeded to MORY for work on the Ammunition Dump.	
ditto	14-5-17	Nothing to report.	
ditto	15-5-17	Personnel of X. Y. & Z/62 T.M.Batteries proceeded to BEHAGNIES for work on the Ammunition Dump.	
ditto	16-5-17 to 31-5-17	Nothing to report.	
	31-5-17.		

[signature]
Lieut. R.F.A.,
D.T.M.O. 62nd. Div. Artillery.

62 DIV

June
1917

Original

Vol 5

<u>Confidential</u>

War Diary

Trench Mortar Batteries

62nd Division

Volume 1

From 1st June 1917
To 30th June 1917

Army Form C. 2118.

TRENCH MORTAR BATTERIES
62ⁿᵈ DIVISION

ORIGINAL

WAR DIARY
or
INTELLIGENCE SUMMARY.

(Erase heading not required.)

Instructions regarding War Diaries and Intelligence Summaries are contained in F. S. Regs., Part II. and the Staff Manual respectively. Title pages will be prepared in manuscript.

Place	Date	Hour	Summary of Events and Information	Remarks and references to Appendices
SAPIGNIES	1-6-17 to 22-6-17		Nothing to report.	
"	23-6-17		X, Y & Z Batteries proceeded to VAULX DUMP to work under 62nd. D.A.C. V. battery proceeded to BEUGNATRE.	
BEUGNATRE	24-6-17 25-6-17		Nothing to report.	
	26-6-17		X Y Z Batteries proceeded to BEUGNATRE.	
	27-6-17 to 30-6-17		Nothing to report	

6-7-17.

J.M. Snell
Lieut RFA.
D.T.M.O. 62nd Div Arty

Secret

Original

Confidential
War Diary
of
62nd Divisional Trench Mortar
Batteries.

Volume VI

From 1st July 1917
To 31st July 1917

Army Form C. 2118.

WAR DIARY
or
INTELLIGENCE SUMMARY

(Erase heading not required.)

Instructions regarding War Diaries and Intelligence Summaries are contained in F.S. Regs., Part II. and the Staff Manual respectively. Title pages will be prepared in manuscript.

D.T.M.O.
2nd DIVISION
No. TM/696/13
Date 1.8.17

Place	Date	Hour	Summary of Events and Information	Remarks and references to Appendices
BEHAGNIES	1-7-17	to	Nothing to report	
"	3-7-17			
"	4-7-17		Trench Mortar Battery proceeded to VAULX	
VAULX	5-7-17	15	Nothing to report	
"	7-7-17		Defensive emplacement to the pan in front of NOREUIL	
"	8-7-17		Nothing to report	
"	9-7-17			
"	10-7-17		Defensive emplacements begun in front of LAGNICOURT	
"	11-7-17	to		
"	19-7-17		Defensive emplacements continued	
"	20-7-17		One 2 inch mortar put in action in the NOREUIL sector	
"	31-7-17	10	Nothing to report	
"	24-7-17			

1-8-17.   [signature]
                           Capt. R.F.A.
                           D.T.M.O. 62nd DIV.

Original

Secret

Vol 7

War Diary

of

62nd Divisional Trench Mortar Batteries

Volume VII

From 1st August 1917.
To 31st August 1917

ORIGINAL

Army Form C. 2118.

62nd. Div. T.M. Bty.

Original

WAR DIARY
INTELLIGENCE SUMMARY

(Erase heading not required.)

Instructions regarding War Diaries and Intelligence Summaries are contained in F. S. Regs., Part II. and the Staff Manual respectively. Title pages will be prepared in manuscript.

Place	Date	Hour	Summary of Events and Information	Remarks and references to Appendices
VAULX	1.8.17 to 7.8.17		Nothing to report.	
BULLECOURT	8.8.17		V/62. T.M. Bty. took over from 7th Div. Arty. Two Medium T.M's in action, one Medium T.M. in reserve, & loaded three over in exchange.	
"	9.8.17		V/62. T.M. Bty. took over from 7th Div. Arty. 1 Heavy Mortar in action.	
"	10.8.17		Nothing to report.	
"			Our 2" fired a few rounds in conjunction with Stokes Mortars, for purpose of testing lines & fires taken out. 10 rounds fired.	
NOREUIL	11.8.17		2" fired on enemy trenches in retaliation for shelling of ours.	
	12.8.17		2 inch fired on enemy trenches with good effect. 23 rounds fired.	
BULLECOURT	13.8.17		Heavy T.M. registered on enemy trench. with good effect. 4 rounds fired.	
-	14.8.17		Nothing to report.	
NOREUIL	15.8.17		2" T.M. fired in conjunction with V.A. Machine Guns & Stokes Mortars on T.M. Emplacements. fired 27 rounds.	
-	16.8.17		2" T.M's fired on enemy trench. T.M.Emplacements/trench with good effect. 6 rounds fired.	
VAULX	16.8.17		Personnel of V/62. T.M. Bty. transferred 6 III Corps.	
NOREUIL	17.8.17		2" T.M's fired on T.M. Emplacement & M.G. post & silenced the Machine Gun. 24 rounds fired.	
BULLECOURT	17.8.17		2" T.M's fired on enemy trenches. 15 rounds fired.	
NOREUIL	18.8.17		2" T.M's engaged enemy Bombing Post, M.G. position & T.M. Emplacement. 28 rounds.	
BULLECOURT	18.8.17		2" T.M.s fired on enemy trenches 43 rounds fired.	

ORIGINAL

Army Form C. 2118.

WAR DIARY
INTELLIGENCE SUMMARY
(Erase heading not required.)

63rd Div. 9th Battn.

Instructions regarding War Diaries and Intelligence Summaries are contained in F. S. Regs., Part II. and the Staff Manual respectively. Title pages will be prepared in manuscript.

Place	Date	Hour	Summary of Events and Information	Remarks and references to Appendices
MOREUIL	19/8/17		One of 2" T.M's engaged T.M. Emplacement & direct hit was obtained and explosion occurred. 42 rounds fired.	
BULLECOURT	19/8/17		2" T.M's fired on T.M. Emplacements 32 rounds fired.	
MOREUIL	20/8/17		Our Medium T.M's engaged enemy T.M. Emplacement + trenches. 33 rounds fired.	
BULLECOURT	20/8/17		2" T.M's in retaliation for F.A. fire on our trenches. 20 rounds fired.	
MOREUIL	21.8.17		Our 2" T.M's engaged enemy T.M. Emplacement with good effect. 80 rounds fired.	
BULLECOURT	21.8.17		Medium T.M's fired on enemys trenches 22 rounds fired.	
MOREUIL	22.8.17		Our 2" T.M's fired on enemys trenches 32 rounds fired.	
BULLECOURT	22.8.17		Our 2" T.M's fired on enemys trenches 25 rounds fired.	
MOREUIL	23.8.17		Nothing to report.	
BULLECOURT	23.8.17		Nothing to report.	
MOREUIL	24.8.17		Fired on enemys trenches 20 rounds fired.	
BULLECOURT	24.8.17		Nothing to report.	
MOREUIL	25.8.17		2" T.M's fired on enemy T.M., trenches + enemy work with other Arty. 45 rounds fired.	
	26.8.17		Nothing to report.	
	27.8.17		2" T.M. fired 10 rounds on suspected T.M. Emplacement.	
	29.8.17			
	30.8.17		Nothing to report.	
	31.8.17			

Capt. RFA

D.T.M.O. 62nd Division.

2/9/17.

Secret.
TM3/19

Reference BMF/1392/9 dated August 5th.

1. At 3 pm on August 8th S/62nd T.M.Bty will take over from the 7th Div Arty, two Medium Trench Mortars in action at U.27.c.60.65, and one Medium Mortar which is in the Dugout at U.20.a.3.5. This dugout marked No 4 will also be taken over and any ammunition at the Guns or in the Bomb store at U.20.a.3.5. S/62nd will supply the guard on this store and will account for all Ammunition dumped there for the 62nd T.M.Bs.

2. S/62nd will hand over three medium Mortars to the 7th Div Arty, time and date will be notified later.

3. At 3pm on August 8th S/62nd T.M.B. will take over from the 7th Div Arty, one Heavy Mortar in action in U.21.c.3.3. and any ammunition with the Gun.
Arrangements will be made between S/62nd and the Heavy T.M.Bty of the 7th Div Arty, as to supplying one guard for the two Guns at U.21.c.3.3. The Officer on duty and half the detachment will sleep at the embankment U.26.c.w.i.

4. The completion of the reliefs will be wired to this Office, using the code word "TOMMY".

5. The present method of ammunition supply in use by the 7th Div Arty will be continued, except that the amount of ammunition, or number of empty trucks required, will always be wired to this Office, as much notice as possible should be given.

Lehmans Lodge.
7th August 1917.

G.A.Powell.
Lieut. R.F.A.
DTMO 62nd Div Arty

Copies 1   S/62nd T.M.Bty
"   2   S/62nd   "   "
"   3   Y/62nd   "   " }
"   4   X/62nd   "   " } For information
"   5-7 DTMO 7th Div   }
"   8-9 War Diary
"   10 File

Original

Vol 8

War Diary
of
62nd Divisional
Trench Mortar Batteries

Volume VIII

From 1st September 1917
To 30th September 1917

Original

Army Form C. 2118.

2nd Div T.M. Btys

WAR DIARY
or
INTELLIGENCE SUMMARY.
(Erase heading not required.)

Instructions regarding War Diaries and Intelligence Summaries are contained in F.S. Regs., Part II. and the Staff Manual respectively. Title pages will be prepared in manuscript.

Place	Date	Hour	Summary of Events and Information	Remarks and references to Appendices
MOREUIL	1/9/17 to 3/9/17		Nothing to report.	
"	4/9/17		2" fired 4 rounds on enemy trenches	
BULLECOURT.	4.9.17		2" registered on enemy trenches 3 rounds fired.	
"	5.9.17		Nothing to report.	
NOREUIL	6.9.17		2" fired 10 rounds on enemy trenches	
"	7.9.17		2" fired 5 rounds on enemy trenches.	
BULLECOURT.	7.9.17		2" fired 3 rounds on cross roads.	
NOREUIL.	8.9.17		2" carried out wire cutting for minor operation which proved very successful 50 rounds fired.	
BULLECOURT.	8.9.17		2" fired 12 rounds on enemy trenches	
NOREUIL	9.9.17		2" fired 32 rounds on enemy wire	
BULLECOURT.	9.9.17.		2" fired 6 rounds on enemy wire.	
NOREUIL	10.9.17		2" co-operated in raid on enemy trenches, fired 46 rounds.	
BULLECOURT.	10.9.17.		2" fired 5 rounds on enemy trenches	
VAULX.	10.9.17.		1/62 T.M.Bty. relieved from 34th Division.	
MORIUIL.	11/9/17		2" carried out wire cutting, several lanes of wire cut, one mortar engaged on suspected MINENWERFER, a large explosion occurred with clouds of white smoke, believed to be ammunition going up. 2" fired at old materials on wire cut in the afternoon. 114 rounds fired.	
BULLECOURT.	11.9.17.		2" carried out wire cutting with Aeroplane observation which proved very satisfactory. & during night fired on enemy trenches. 21 rounds fired.	
NOREUIL	12.9.17		2" completed wire cutting and co-operated in raid on enemy trenches 40 rounds fired.	

A 5834 Wt. W4973/M687 750,000 8/16 D. D. & L. Ltd. Forms/C.2118/13.

Original

Army Form C. 2118.

Instructions regarding War Diaries and Intelligence Summaries are contained in F. S. Regs., Part II. and the Staff Manual respectively. Title pages will be prepared in manuscript.

WAR DIARY
or
INTELLIGENCE SUMMARY.
(Erase heading not required.)

Place	Date	Hour	Summary of Events and Information	Remarks and references to Appendices
BULLECOURT	12.9.17		2" bombarded enemy trenches. 64 rounds fired.	
MOREUIL	13.9.17		2" fired 4 rounds on enemy trench.	
VAULX	14.9.17		Personnel & guns of 3/4 7/62 were loaned to 50th Division to assist in a special operation.	
MOREUIL	15.9.17		2" fired 19 rounds on enemy mine.	
"	16.9.17		2" fired on suspected M.G. emplacement 25 rounds fired.	
"	17.9.17		2" fired 27 rounds on enemy trenches.	
VAULX	18.9.17		2" fired 19 rounds on suspected enemy emplacements.	
MOREUIL	19.9.17		2/7/62 returned from 50th Division.	
"	19.9.17		This fired 20 rounds on enemy post.	
"	20.9.17		2" fired 47 rounds on enemy posts, a direct hit was obtained.	
MOREUIL	21.9.17		2" fired 11 rounds in retaliation to enemy's fire.	
"	22.9.17		2" fired 5 rounds on enemy trench	
"	23.9.17		Nothing to report.	
"	24.9.17			
"	25.9.17		9·45" + 2" carried out a concentrated bombardment on enemy front & support line, result appeared to be very satisfactory, it is believed great destruction was done, 2" fired 203 rounds + 9·45" fired 20 rounds.	
"	26.9.17		2" fired 8 rounds on enemy trench.	
"	27.9.17		9·45" + 2" carried out bombardment on enemy trenches 9·45" fired 20 rounds 2" 444.	
BULLECOURT	27.9.17		2" fired 10 rounds on enemy trench.	
"	28.9.17		2" fired 5 rounds on enemy trench.	
VAULX	28.9.17		Personnel of 7/62. proceeded to III Corps T.M. School for course on 6" T.M's.	
BULLECOURT	29.9.17		2" fired 5 rounds on enemy trench	
"	30.9.17		2" fired 11 rounds on enemy trench	

J.W. Snell
Capt R.F.A.
T.M.O. 62nd Division
2/10/17.

62 Div

October
1917

Secret   Original

Vol 9

War Diary

of

62nd Divisional Trench

Mortar Batteries

Volume IX

From 1st October 1917
To 31st October 1917

Original

Army Form C. 2118.

62nd Divisional
Trench Mortar Batteries

WAR DIARY
or
INTELLIGENCE SUMMARY.
(Erase heading not required.)

Instructions regarding War Diaries and Intelligence Summaries are contained in F. S. Regs., Part II. and the Staff Manual respectively. Title pages will be prepared in manuscript.

Place	Date	Hour	Summary of Events and Information	Remarks and references to Appendices
VAULX.	1.10.17.		Nothing to report.	
MEAULTE.	2.10.17.		9.45" fired 15 rounds on Enemy Trenches. 2" also fired on enemy trenches.	
–	3.10.17.		9.45" & 2" shell bombarded enemy trenches.	
–	4.10.17.		2" & 9.45" fired 10 rounds into BIENCOURT.	
BULLECOURT.	5.10.17.		2" fired 15 rounds on enemy trenches.	
BAPAUME.	6.10.17.		9.45" fired 20 rounds on enemy O.P.	
–	7.10.17.		9.45" & 2" carried out concentrated bombardment on enemy trenches. 9.45" fired 20 – 2" 90.	
BULLECOURT.	8.10.17.		Wire cutting carried out. Wire cutting with good results. 9.45" engaged enemy T.M.	
–	9.10.17.		2"M fired 10 rounds on enemy trenches.	
–	10.10.17.		Nothing to report.	
MOREUIL.	10.10.17.		9.45" silenced enemy Minenwerfer and fired on enemy snipers. 2" engaged suspected M.G. at or near corner of the infantry. 2" fired 14 – the 9.45" fired 70.	
BULLECOURT.	11.10.17.		Wire cutting carried out. by 2". 139 rounds fired.	
–	12.10.17.		Nothing to report.	
MOREUIL.	13.10.17.		9.45" fired 20 rounds on enemy trenches.	
–	14.10.17.		9.45" fired 10 rounds on cross roads to Enemy Trenches. 2" fired 12 rounds on Enemy front line.	
–	15.10.17.		Personnel of T.M.B. proceeded to 3rd Army Trench Mortar School for a course on the 6" STOKES.	
–	16.10.17.		9.45" engaged enemy T.M. & 2" fired in retaliation for enemy fire.	
–	17.10.17.		9.45" engaged enemy T.M. & also fired into NOREUIL. 149 rounds fired.	
BULLECOURT.	17.10.17.		2" retaliated	
MOREUIL.	18.10.17.		9.45" fired 20 rounds on enemy T.M.	
VAULX.	17.10.17.		V & Z batteries were relieved by Z Mortars & proceeded to Rest Camps at MEAULTE.	
BAPAUME.	20.10.17.		Nothing to report.	
–	25.10.17.		Personnel of VxYxZ were attached to Inf. of Divisions for instruction work or employment.	
–	26.10.17.		Nothing to report.	
–	27.10.17.		Nothing to report.	
–	29.10.17.		4.62 T.M.Bty. returned from I.M. School.	
–	30.10.17.			
–	31.10.17.		Nothing to report.	

B. Carroll
Captain.
T.M.O. 62nd Division.

Original

Vol 10

War Diary

of

62nd Divisional Trench Mortar Batteries

Volume X

From 1st November 1914
To 30th November 1914

Original

Army Form C. 2118.

Instructions regarding War Diaries and Intelligence Summaries are contained in F. S. Regs., Part II. and the Staff Manual respectively. Title pages will be prepared in manuscript.

WAR DIARY
or
INTELLIGENCE SUMMARY.
(Erase heading not required.)

Trench Mortar Batteries 62nd Division.

Place	Date	Hour	Summary of Events and Information	Remarks and references to Appendices
BAPAUME	1/4/17 to 6/4/17		Nothing to report.	
"	7/4/17		T.M. Personnel returned from 2nd & 4th Divisions	
"	8/4/17		Personnel of 1/62 proceeded to 36th Divn at FAUVILLCOURT.	
"	9/4/17		Personnel of 1 x V + 2 T.M.Bs proceeded to 36th Division at FAUVILLCOURT.	
FAUVILLCOURT	10/4/17		Nothing to report.	
"	11/4/17		Personnel reworking on Gun Positions + carrying Ammunition took over 3 9.45inch + 2 6inch TMs from 36th Division.	
"	12/4/17			
"	13/4/17 14/4/17 15/4/17		Nothing to report.	
"	16/4/17 17/4/17		9.45" fired on MARTINPUICH village and back fired on enemys trenches. 6" fired on enemys trenches.	
"	18/4/17 19/4/17 20/4/17		9.45" + 6" fired in the afternoon according to programme.	
"	21/4/17		Nothing to report.	
"	22/4/17 30/4/17			

Marett
D.T.M.O. 62nd Division

A.8431 Wt. W4973/M687 750,000 8/16 D. D. & L. Ltd. Forms/C.2118/13.

62nd F.M.B.

December 1917.

Army Form C. 2118.

WAR DIARY
or
~~INTELLIGENCE SUMMARY~~

Trench Mortar Batteries. 62nd Division. ORIGINAL.

Instructions regarding War Diaries and Intelligence Summaries are contained in F. S. Regs., Part II. and the Staff Manual respectively. Title pages will be prepared in manuscript.

(Erase heading not required.)

Place	Date	Hour	Summary of Events and Information	Remarks and references to Appendices
RAYAULCOURT.	1/12/17 to 21/12/17.		Nothing to report.	
"	22/12/17.		All T.M.Personnel proceeded to CAUCHIN LEGAL.	
CAUCHIN LEGAL.	23/12/17 to 31/12/17.		Nothing to report.	

E.M.Murphy. Lieut R.F.A.
for D.T.M.O. 62nd Division.

ORIGINAL.

WAR DIARY OF
62ND DIVISIONAL TRENCH MORTAR BATTERIES.

VOLUME - XIII

FROM 1st JANUARY 1918.
TO 31st JANUARY 1918.

[signed] Powell
Captain R.F.A.
D.T.M.O. 62nd Division.

ORIGINAL

Army Form C. 2118.

WAR DIARY
INTELLIGENCE SUMMARY
of 62nd Div. Trench Mortar Battery

Instructions regarding War Diaries and Intelligence Summaries are contained in F. S. Regs., Part II. and the Staff Manual respectively. Title pages will be prepared in manuscript.

(Erase heading not required.)

Place	Date	Hour	Summary of Events and Information	Remarks and references to Appendices
Gouchin Légal	Jan 1st		Nothing to Report	
	2nd		All T.M. Personnel proceeded to Camblyneul	
Camblyneul	3rd to 7th		Nothing to Report	
Roclincourt	8th		All T.M. Personnel proceeded to Roclincourt. Took over 1-9.45"T.M. & 8-6Inch T.Ms. from 56th Division.	
	9th to 15th		Nothing to Report.	
	16th		6 Inch T.Ms bombarded enemy trenches.	
	17th		6 Inch T.Ms — do —	
	18th to 21st		Nothing to Report.	
	22nd		6 Inch T.Ms bombarded enemy trenches	
	23rd to 25th		Nothing to Report	
	26th		6 Inch T.Ms co-operated with Field guns in concentrated bombardment of enemy trenches & strong points	
	27th		Nothing to Report	
	28th		6 Inch T.M. bombarded enemy trenches	
	29th		— do —	
	30th		— do —	
	31st		— do —	

Capt.
CAPT. R.F.A.
D.T.M.O. 62nd DIVN.

ORIGINAL. *Confidential*

WAR DIARY OF

62nd DIVISIONAL TRENCH MORTAR BATTERIES.

VOLUME .13.

From February 1st 1918
TO   February 28th 1918.

4, 3, 18.
                                    [signature] Captain R.F.A.
                                     A/D.T.M.O. 62nd Division.

Original

Army Form C. 2118.

WAR DIARY
or
INTELLIGENCE SUMMARY.
(Erase heading not required.)

Trench Mortar Batteries
62nd Division.

Instructions regarding War Diaries and Intelligence Summaries are contained in F. S. Regs., Part II. and the Staff Manual respectively. Title pages will be prepared in manuscript.

Place	Date	Hour	Summary of Events and Information	Remarks and references to Appendices
ROCLINCOURT	1/2	-	Nothing to report.	
"	2/2	-	6inch fired on enemy support trenches	
"	3/2	-	9.45inch bombarded CAVRELLE and 6inch fired on enemy trenches.	
"	4/2	-	6inch fired on enemy T.M. Emplacements	
"	5/2	-	6inch fired on enemy. wire & suspected mine.	
"	6/2	-	6inch engaged enemy T.M.	
"	7/2	-	6inch fired on enemy wire	
"	8/2	-	6inch fired on enemy trenches	
"	9/2	-	6inch fired on enemy wire	
"	10/2	-	All Batteries relieved by 5oth. T.M.Bs and proceeded to CAMBLIGNEUL.	
"	11/2	-	Reorganisation of T.M.Bs and 17 KOR Gunners transferred to V/31.	
"	12/2 & 28/2/3.	-	Nothing to report.	
	5/3/3.			

C. R. Osborne Capt. RFA
V/61. T.M.O. 62nd Division.

62ND Divisional Artillery.

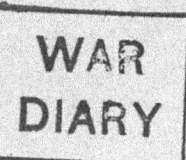

D.T.M.O.

62nd DIVISION

MARCH 1918

ORIGINAL.

WAR DIARY.

Trench Mortar Batteries.   62nd Division.

VOLUMNE 3.

From March 1st 18.
To   March 31st 18.

ORIGINAL

Instructions regarding War Diaries and Intelligence
Summaries are contained in F.S. Regs., Part II.
and the Staff Manual respectively. Title pages
will be prepared in manuscript.

WAR DIARY
or
INTELLIGENCE SUMMARY.
(Erase heading not required.)

Trench Mortar Batteries.
62nd Division.

Place	Date	Hour	Summary of Events and Information	Remarks and references to Appendices
GAMBLIGNEUL.	1/3 to 6/3		Resting; nothing to report.	
	7/3		Our T.M.Bs relieved the 31st Div T.M.Bs and also engaged enemy T.M.'s.	
ROCLINCOURT.	8/3		6inch T.Ms fired on enemy T.Ms and also on Trench Junction.	
"	9/3		6 inch fired on enemy T.M.	
"	10/3		6 inch fired on enemy T.M.	
"	11/3		6 inch fired on enemy front line and also engaged enemy Minnie.	
"	12/3		6 inch fired on enemy trenches also engaged enemy T.M.	
"	13/3		Nothing to report.	
"	14/3		6 inch fired on enemy wire.	
"	15/3		6 inch fired on enemy wire and cut two gaps.	
"	16/3		6 inch fired on enemy wire and engaged enemy Machine Gun.	
"	17/3		6 inch carried out wire cutting and cut gap at T.24.d.67.10 also registered M.G. at T.24.d.	
"	18/3 to 23/3		Nothing to report.	
	24/3		All T.M.Personnel relieved by 3rd Canadian T.M.Bs and proceeded to BERLES.	
BERLES	25/3 to 30/3		Nothing to report.	
"	31/3		Personnel of Trench Mortar Batteries proceeded to SOUASTRE.	

31/3/18.

Captain R.F.A.
D.T.M.O. 62nd Division.

62nd Divisional Artillery

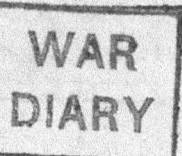

DIVISIONAL TRENCH MORTAR OFFICER

62nd DIVISION

APRIL 1 9 1 8

Original

JA/15

VOLUMNE. 4/6

Trench Mortar Batteries

62nd. Division

From. April 1st. 18.
To. April 30th. 18.

C R Bottomley Capt. R.F.A.
D.T.M.O. 62nd. Division

1. 5. 18.

Trench Mortar Batteries.
62nd Division.

INTELLIGENCE SUMMARY

Place	Date	Hour	Summary of Events and Information	Remarks and references to Appendices
SOUASTRE	1/4/18		Positions reconnoitred in GOMMECOURT - BIEZ WOOD.	
"	2/4/18		Personnel proceeded from SOUASTRE to forward billets in GOMMECOURT and commenced work on positions in front of ROSSIGNOL WOOD.	
GOMMECOURT	3/4 to 5/4		Work proceeding on positions above stated.	
"	6/4/18		Fired 30 rounds in operations in ROSSIGNOL WOOD area.	
"	7/4/18		Work proceeding on positions.	
"	8/4/18		Captain J.B.Powell on posting to 310th Bde R.F.A. handed over Command of 62nd Divl Trench Mortars to Captain G.R.Bottomley.	
"	9/4/18		Work proceeding on positions.	
"	10/4/18		Relieved by 37th Divl T.Ms. Personnel withdrew to SOUASTRE.	
SOUASTRE.	11/4/18		Positions reconnoitred in BUCQUOY area by D.T.M.O. and Battery Commanders.	
MONCHY au BOIS.	12/4/18		Personnel proceeded to forward billets in CHEMIN des DAMES near MONCHY au BOIS and commenced work.	
"	13th to 25th.		Work p-roceeding. 12 Guns put into action in the sector, 4 being in forward positions, 4 in defensive, and 4 in PURPLE LINE defence positions.	
"	17/4/18		Fired 33 rounds in conjunction with Field and Heavy Artillery	
"	26/4/18		Relieved in the line by 37th Divisional T.M's. 12 guns handed over in action. Personnel withdrew to AUTHIE.	
AUTHIE.	27th to 30th.		Training in progress.	

Original.   Confidential
　　　　　　War Diary.

Trench Mortar Batteries
62nd. Division.
─────

Volume 17

From May 1st. 1918.
To.   May. 31st. 1918.

　　　　　　　　　　A R Bottomley Captain R.F.A.
　　　　　　　　　　D.T.M.O. 62nd. Division

2nd. June. 1918.

Original

Army Form C. 2118.

WAR DIARY
or ~~INTELLIGENCE SUMMARY~~
(Erase heading not required.)

Trench Mortar Batteries.
62nd Division.

VOLUME 5.

Instructions regarding War Diaries and Intelligence Summaries are contained in F. S. Regs., Part II. and the Staff Manual respectively. Title pages will be prepared in manuscript.

Place	Date	Hour	Summary of Events and Information	Remarks and references to Appendices
AUTHIE.	1/5/18		Personnel resting. Training in Musketry, Gas, Bombing etc proceeding.	
" "	2/5 to 3/5		Nothing to report.	
" "	4/5/18		Personnel working on Rifle ranges in AUTHIE district under orders of 62nd Division.	
" "	5/5/18 to 12/5/18		Nothing to report.	
" "	13/5/18		One section of X/62 reported to N.Z.Division for duty. (To man two guns). Y/62 Trench Mortar Battery complete move up into 37th Divisional Area to man guns under D.T.M.O. 37th Division.	
" "	14/5/18		One section of X/62 reported to 57th D.T.M.O. for duty. (To man two guns).	
" "	15/5/18		Nothing to report.	
" "	16/5/18		62nd Division taking over left sector. 37th T.Ms remain in action under D.T.M.O. 37th and Y/62 and X/62 carry on under D.T.M.O. 62nd Division.	
" "	17/5/18		Section of X/62 under N.Z. Division put in two offensive guns at (57.d.N.E) K.21.a.5.3.	
" "	18/5/18		Nothing to report.	
" "	19/5/18		Rear H.Q. and Q.M.Stores move from AUTHIE to J.2.b.5.3. Section of X/62 under 57th Division put in two defensive guns at (57d.N.E) E.27.d.8.3.	
" "	20/5/18		Section of X/62 attached N.Z.Division fired 200 rounds covering a raid by Infantry.	
COUIN.	21/5 to 31/5		This Section fired about 50 rounds a day on enemy trenches etc.	
" "	20/5 to 3/5		Y/62 put in 6 defensive guns, two at (57d.N.E.) E.24.c.7.2. and 4 at F.20.b.4.2.	
" "	26/5/18		Section of X/62 under 62nd Division.put in two offensive guns at (57d.N.E.) F.22.d.4.9.	
" "	31/5/18.		X/62 fire 20 rounds on suspected T.M. at ABLAINZEVILLE at night. Enemy under the impression that the bombs were dropped by an Aeroplane and switched on several searchlights over that town.	
	2/6/18.			

E.R.B. *[signature]* Captain R.F.A.
D.T.M.O. 62nd Division.

Original.

Vol 17

War Diary.

62nd. Divisional Trench Mortars
62nd. Division.

Volume 6/18

From June 1st. 1918.
To. June 30th. 1918.

R Bottomley Captain R.F.A.
D.T.M.O. 62nd Division

July. 2nd. 18.

Original.

Army Form C. 2118.

WAR DIARY
or
~~INTELLIGENCE~~ SUMMARY
(Erase heading not required.)

Trench Mortar Batteries.
62nd Division.

Volume W.4.18

Place	Date	Hour	Summary of Events and Information	Remarks and references to Appendices
COUIN.	1/6/18.		X/62 had two guns in action at (57D NW) F.22.d.4.9. and two defensive guns under the Centre Division and two offensive guns under the Right Division of the Corps.	
"	"		X/62 had six guns in action in defensive positions in the Left (62) Division.	
"	2/6/18		X/62 fired 20 rounds on hostile Trench Mortars, Trenches and Strong points.	
"	3/6/18		X/62 fired 20 rounds.	
"			X/62 fired 40 rounds in conjunction with Heavy and Field Artillery concentration on ABLAINZEVILLE.	
"	4/6/18		X/62 fired 40 rounds on hostile trench mortar, silencing it.	
"	5/6/18		Nothing to report.	
"	6/6/18		X/62 fired 20 rounds on hostile machine guns.	
"	7/6/18		X/62 fired 20 rounds on enemy T.M. The positions were shelled from the Right Rear.	
"	8/6/18		X/62 fired 10 rounds on new work at the request of the Infantry.	
"	9/6/18		X/62 fired 30 rounds on hostile Trench Mortars and Machine Guns.	
"	10/6/18		Nothing to report.	
"	11/6/18		X/62 fired 30 rounds on suspected O.P. and hostile T.M.	
"	12/6/18		X/62 fired 20 rounds on hostile Trench Mortars in retaliation.	
"	13/6/18		Nothing to report.	
"	14/6/18		X/62 fired 50 rounds on hostile Trench Mortar, silencing it.	
"	15/6/18		Nothing to report.	
"	16/6/18		X/62 fired 10 rounds on trenches.	
"	17/6/18 to 18/6/18		Nothing to report.	
"	19/6/18		X/62 fired 20 rounds on hostile Trench Mortars which ceased firing immediately.	
"	20/6/18		X/62 fired 20 rounds on hostile Trench Mortar.	
"	21/6/18		X/62 fired 25 rounds on hostile M.G. Emplacements.	
"	22/6/18		X/62 fired 20 rounds on hostile Trench Mortars.	
"	23/6/18		X/62 fired 30 rounds on hostile Trench Mortars.	
"	24/6/18		X/62 fired 20 rounds on hostile Machine Guns.	
"	25/6/18		62nd Divl Trench Mortars were relieved in the line in all Sectors by 37th Divl T.M's and proceeded by lorry and horse transport to Rest Billets in ORVILLE.	
ORVILLE.	26/6/18 to 30/6/18		Steady training commences, including Rifle Shooting and Bombing. Training in progress.	

W Shone, Captain R.F.A
D.T.M.O. 62nd Division

Divl. Artillery

62nd Division.

62nd DIVISION TRENCH MORTAR BATTERIES

J U L Y, 1 9 1 8.

Original:

War Diary.

Trench Mortar Batteries
62nd Division

From July 1st 1918
To July 31st 1918

Volume 7.

August 7th. 18.

C.R. Bottomley Captain R.F.A.
D.T.M.O. 62nd Division

ORIGINAL

Army Form C. 2118.

Trench Mortar Bttrs
63rd Division Volume 6

WAR DIARY
or
INTELLIGENCE SUMMARY.
(Erase heading not required.)

Instructions regarding War Diaries and Intelligence Summaries are contained in F.S. Regs., Part II. and the Staff Manual respectively. Title pages will be prepared in manuscript.

Place	Date	Hour	Summary of Events and Information	Remarks and references to Appendices
ORVILLE	July 1 to 14		Training in progress.	
"	15th		Both Batteries proceeded by train to French Dump Area at ARCIS.	
ARCIS	16 to 18th		Nothing to report.	
"	19th		Both batteries proceeded by road to EPERNAY.	
MUTIGNY	20th		Both batteries proceeded by road to GERMAINE for work on the Railheads.	
			Ammunition Dumps.	
GERMAINE	20 to 29th		Work proceeding on Dumps.	
"	29th		H.Q. moved by road to CHALONS-sur-MARNE and entrained thence for ALTHIE in IV Corps (British) Area	
"	29th		X/62 attached to S.A.A. Section 62nd Div. at CADRAN Cross Roads	
"	30 & 31st		Nothing to report.	

August 3rd 18.

A.R.Rowley Captain R.A.
A.T.M.O. 62nd Division

Original

Vol 20

War Diary

of

62nd Divisional Ammunition Column

Volume XX

From 1st August 1918
To 31st August 1918

WAR DIARY or INTELLIGENCE SUMMARY

Army Form C. 2118.

AUGUST 1908 ORIGINAL

Instructions regarding War Diaries and Intelligence Summaries are contained in F.S. Regs., Part II. and the Staff Manual respectively. Title pages will be prepared in manuscript.

(Erase heading not required.)

Place	Date	Hour	Summary of Events and Information	Remarks and references to Appendices
Aigny Chatow	1/5/18	8 am	Spent another day at AIGNY resting and cleaning up	—
	2/6/18	7 pm	DAC less SAA Section marched to CHALONS and entrained departed at 12.30 noon	—
Lucheux	3/6/18	5 pm	Detrained at DOULLENS at 5pm marched HQ to AUTHIE, 1 & 2 Sections to St LEDGER-LES-AUTHIE	—
	4/6/18	7 pm	HQ DAC moved to St LEDGER-LES-AUTHIE I 11.6.5.E.	—
	5/5/18	5 pm	SAA Section arrived under orders of DAC established PAS-GAUDIEMPRE ROAD C.17.6.6. 9 T reinforcements	—
			Arrived from RA Reinforcement Camp at ARMY. 41 to 310 Bde. A.24.313 Bde 15th DAC	—
	6/6/18	5 pm	Resting, Wagons inspected by I.O.M.	—
	7/5/18	5 pm	" Lieut McGLASHAN & RAFE personnel attached to No 1 Section	—
	8/8/18	5 pm	" 1 O.R. reinforcement to 310 Bde Inspection of S.B. Magazines by D.C.O. T.M. Personnel	—
			withdrawn from SAA Section. 20 O.R. from 1 & 2 Section attached to SAA Section LIEUT	—
			LEE Sinclair Adams arrived from BASE posted to SAA Section	—
	9/6/18	5 pm	Lightning T.M. Rotation Training & Drilling re-commenced. LIEUT McGLASHAN R.E.	—
			by LIEUT CLARKSON R.E inspection by G.O.C.R.A.	—
	10/5/18	5 pm	LIEUT. COL FA WOODCOCK, DSO proceeded on leave to UK. CAPT J FRASER assumes Command	—
			11 O.R. reinforcements arrive posted 4 to 310 Bde, 7 to 313 Bde Supplying T.M. Ration	—
			and training. 27 MULES arrived and posted to No 2 Section	—

Army Form C. 2118.

ORIGINAL

WAR DIARY
or
INTELLIGENCE SUMMARY.
(Erase heading not required.)

Instructions regarding War Diaries and Intelligence Summaries are contained in F. S. Regs., Part II. and the Staff Manual respectively. Title pages will be prepared in manuscript.

AUGUST 1915

Place	Date	Hour	Summary of Events and Information	Remarks and references to Appendices
Ref Map 5¾ D 1/40,000	11/8/15	5pm	Church Parade. Relieving T.M. actions. 21 O.R. Reinforcement arrived 6 to 312 B⁵⁺ 15 to 310 B⁵⁺	1
	12/8/15	5pm	Deliveries. T.M. actions. Training & Drilling	2
	13/8/15	5pm	"	3
	14/8/15	5pm	11 B.S. wagons to 11th Capt. AGRICULTURE OFFICER	4
			18 L.D. horses ammn. prods. arr. & to No.1 Section & to No. 2 Section 55 to S.A.A Section	5
				" "
			10 to No.3 Section. 60 Indian reinforcement arrived and took up fatigues	
	15/8/15	6pm	Deliveries. T.M. actions. Training. Received urgent demand for Ammunition turned out echelons of No. 1 & 2 Sections & delivered to the Guns	6
	16/8/15	5pm	Supplying Ammunition. echelons of 1 & 2 Sections turned out & delivered to the Guns. Returned T.M. actions. Establish A.R.P & II.17 c. 9.9. Lieut OWEN 70 & 30 O.R. T.M.R. 6. 3/2 Mds 5. DAC 10 (5 to No.1 Section & 5 to S.A.A.Section)	7
			35 reinforcement arrived 310 B⁵⁺ to	
	17/8/15	5pm	Supplying Ammunition to Guns & T.M. Returned T.M. actions	"
	18/8/15	5pm	"	" (2/Lt BIRRELL I.S.)
	19/8/15	5pm	"	" 1 Officer + 5 O.R. reinforcement arrived
	20/8/15	5pm	"	" 7/Lt. BIRRELL posted to 310 B⁵⁺
	21/8/15	5am	"	" 3 O.R. reinforcement
			arrvs. spool 1 to DTMR 1 to 310 B⁵⁺ + 1 to 312 B⁵⁺	

WAR DIARY
or
INTELLIGENCE SUMMARY.

Army Form C. 2118.

AUGUST 1915

ORIGINAL

Place	Date	Hour	Summary of Events and Information	Remarks and references to Appendices
Ref Map 57.D 1/40,000	22/8/15	5pm	D.A.C. 600 SAA Section moved to east of SOUASTRE H.22.a.7.2. LIEUT OWEN and 1 O.R. attached to 5th DIV. A.R.P. West of FONQUEVILLERS E.21.b.7.9. Both teams turned out to supply 500 rounds per gun at Battery positions. Believing T.M. activity.	Lieut Capt RFA [signatures]
	23/8/15	5pm	Supplying Ammunition and relieving T.M. section and fatigued LIEUT. OWEN returns to old A.R.P.	
	24/8/15	7am	D.A.C. 600 S.A.A. Section moved to TOUTENCOURT at 6am. Left TOUTENCOURT at 2pm + proceeded to HARPONVILLE. Supplying Ammunition. 1 S Wagon and Team left with T.M.B. at AUTHIE. S.A.A. Section under orders of Q Division	
	25/8/15	8pm	Left HARPONVILLE at 4pm and moved to V.6.d. Lieut OWEN + 20 O.R's A.R.P. at new track V.13.C. Lieut.Col. F.A WOODCOCK. D.S.O. supplying Ammunition. M.O. and proceeded on tomorrow. at new track V.13.C. Lieut.Col. F.A WOODCOCK. D.S.O. actions from team and ammunition LIEUT L WILSON assumed D.A.C. supplying Ammunition 7 Indian O.R. wounded 3 Mules wounded	fao fao fao
	26/8/15	8pm	" " moved to X.15.a.9.5	fao
	27/8/15	8pm	" "	fao
	28/8/15	8pm	" "	fao
57.C 57.D.0.0.0	29/8/15	8pm	" Loaded Ammunition wagon out of new ANCRE at ALBERT and others came to D/312 moved to S.14.C.2.6	fao

AUGUST 1918   ORIGINAL

Army Form C. 2118.

WAR DIARY
or
INTELLIGENCE SUMMARY.
(Erase heading not required.)

Instructions regarding War Diaries and Intelligence Summaries are contained in F. S. Regs., Part II. and the Staff Manual respectively. Title pages will be prepared in manuscript.

Place	Date	Hour	Summary of Events and Information	Remarks and references to Appendices
Rd Bugs 57c 1/40,000	30/8/18	5 pm	Supplying Ammunition & Rations, old Gun Position	two
	31/8/5	5 pm	" " " "	two

Meercloek Mp. 60
map 62.b.u.
(my)

Original.

War Diary.

Trench Mortar Batteries
62nd Division

Volume XXI

From Sept. 1st 1918
To Sept. 30th 1918

G. Murphy Captain R.F.A.
D.T.M.O. 62nd Division

Oct. 3rd. 18.

Army Form C. 2118.

WAR DIARY
or
INTELLIGENCE SUMMARY.
(Erase heading not required.)

Travel Motor Bus 62nd Division

Title pages Volume 9.

Instructions regarding War Diaries and Intelligence Summaries are contained in F. S. Regs., Part II. and the Staff Manual respectively. Title pages will be prepared in manuscript.

Place	Date	Hour	Summary of Events and Information	Remarks and references to Appendices
GOMIECOURT	1/9 & 7/9		Nothing to report.	
"	8/9		Both batteries moved by road to BEUGNY, personnel of X & Y Batteries proceeded to BERTINCOURT for work on Ammunition Dumps.	
"	9 to 25th		Nothing to report.	
BEUGNY	26th		Personnel of Y/62 attached to 310, 312th Brigades for duty.	
"	27th		Y/62 working on Ammunition Dumps.	
"	28th		Battery HQRs moved by road to RUYALCOURT.	
RUYALCOURT	29th		Nothing to report.	
"	30th		Both batteries moved by road to HAVRINCOURT.	

Dec. 3rd 1918

G. Mayler, Captain RFA
D.T.M.O. 62nd Division

No 21 Original.

War Diary.

Trench Mortar Btties
62nd Division

Volume No. 22

From Oct 1st. 1918.
To. Oct 31st 1918.

A.R.Bolton, Captain RFA.
D.T.M.O. 62nd Division

Nov 5th. 18.

Original.

WAR DIARY
INTELLIGENCE SUMMARY

Trench Mortar Batteries 62nd Division

Army Form C. 2118.

Volume 10.

Place	Date	Hour	Summary of Events and Information	Remarks and references to Appendices
HAVRINCOURT	1/10/18		Personnel working on Ammunition Dump	
"	2/10		Both batteries proceeded by road to MASNIERES	
MASNIERES	3/10		Nothing to report	
"	4/10		Batteries proceeded to CREVECOEUR	
CREVECOEUR	5/10		Nothing to report	
"	6/10		Batteries proceeded to CATTENIERES	
"	7/10		Both batteries proceeded by road to BEAUVOIS	
BEAUVOIS	8/10		T.M. positions @ SOLESMES reconnoitred and chosen	
"	9/10		Detachments from X/62 proceeded to Railway Embankment and put in two Guns	
"	10/10		2am X/62 cooperated with other Artillery in barrage preceding attack on SOLESMES from SOLESMES Road	
"			5.30 am dets. Y/62 to remainder of X/62 proceeded to dumps on the QUARRY - SOLESMES Road	
"			Personnel with horses from SOLESMES position	
QUARRY	23/10		Nothing to report	
"	24/10		Batteries proceeded to ST DENNIS	
"	25/10		Nothing to report	
ST DENNIS	26/10		All personnel with B.A.C of F.A. Brigades withdrawn to T.M. Camp	
"	27/10		Training in progress	
	28/10			

W.M.Shann
D.T.M.O. Captain R.F.A.
62nd Division

Original

Vol 22

War Diary.

62nd. Trench Mortar Bties;
62nd. Division

Volume II.

From. Nov. 1st. 18
To. Nov. 30th. 18.

A.R.Bohomley, Captain RFA
D.T.M.O. 62nd Division

Dec 3rd 18.

Original.

Trench Mortar Blues
62nd Division

Army Form C. 2118.

WAR DIARY
or
INTELLIGENCE SUMMARY.
(Erase heading not required.)

Instructions regarding War Diaries and Intelligence Summaries are contained in F. S. Regs., Part II. and the Staff Manual respectively. Title pages will be prepared in manuscript.

Volume 11.

Place	Date	Hour	Summary of Events and Information	Remarks and references to Appendices
ST. PYTHON	Nov 1st to 2nd		Training in progress.	
"	3rd.		2/62 put 8 Trench Mortars in/c ORSINVAL.	
"	4th.		4/62 co-operated with other Artillery in the bombardment preceding the attack on ORSINVAL. Remainder moved to ESCARMAIN.	
ESCARMAIN	5th.		Nothing to report.	
"	6th.		Personnel of both batteries moved by road to FRASNOY.	
FRASNOY	7th.		Nothing to report.	
"	8th.		X + Y Btties moved by road to LE CARNOY.	
LE CARNOY	9th.		Moved by road to HARCHIES.	
HARCHIES	10th.		Nothing to report.	
"	11th.		Batteries moved by road to NEUF MESNIL. Hostilities ceased.	
NEUF MESNIL	12th to 16th		Nothing to report.	
"	17th.		Moved by road to SOUS LE BOIS.	
SOUS LE BOIS	18th.		Nothing to report.	
"	19th.		Personnel moved to ST PYTHON and joined the 61st Divisional Reception Camp.	
ST PYTHON	20th to 30th.		Training in progress.	

8/12/18.

R B Wheeler Captain R.F.A.
D.T.M.O. 62nd Division.

Original

CONFIDENTIAL

War Diary.

Trench Mortar Btties
62nd Division

Volume 12

From Dec. 1st. 18
To Dec. 31st. 18.

A. Brooks

Captain R.F.A.
D.T.M.O. 62nd Division

2/1/19

Original.

Trench Mortar Offr
62nd Division

Volume 12

Army Form C. 21

WAR DIARY
or
INTELLIGENCE SUMMARY.
(Erase heading not required.)

Instructions regarding War Diaries and Intelligence Summaries are contained in F. S. Regs., Part II. and the Staff Manual respectively. Title pages will be prepared in manuscript.

Place	Date	Hour	Summary of Events and Information	Remarks and references to Appendices
ST PYTON	1/12/18		Training in progress.	
"	2/12/18		Personnel of TMBs moved with the 62nd Div. Reception Corps to Cambrai.	
CAMBRAI	8.12.18 to 22.12.18		Training in progress.	
"	23.12.18		Moved by train to Euskirchen.	
EUSKIRCHEN	24.12.18		Arrived at Euskirchen.	
"	25.12.18		Nothing to report.	
"	26.12.18		The Div. reformed Division at OEFF.	
"	29.12.18		Training in progress	
OEFF	26.12.18 to 30.12.18			
"	31.12.18		40 O.R. attached to F.17 Brigade for duty.	

D.T.M.O. 62nd Division

Captain, RFA

Army Form C. 2118.

ORIGINAL COPY WAR DIARY
or
INTELLIGENCE SUMMARY.
(Erase heading not required.)

Trench Mortar Batteries
62nd Division

JANUARY

WO 95 2 4

Place	Date	Hour	Summary of Events and Information	Remarks and references to Appendices
OLEF.	1-1-19		2 O.Rs. from X/62. attached to 310th Bde.	
-	1-1-19		2 ORs. from X/62 attached to 312th Bde.	
	2-1-19		Nothing to report.	
	3-1-19			

H. Bowser
Capt. R.F.A.
D.T.M.O. 62nd Division.

Original

Army Form C. 2118.

Trench Mortar Batteries.
62nd Division

Vol 2 3

WAR DIARY
or
INTELLIGENCE SUMMARY.
(Erase heading not required.)

Army Form C. 2118.

Instructions regarding War Diaries and Intelligence Summaries are contained in F. S. Regs., Part II. and the Staff Manual respectively. Title pages will be prepared in manuscript.

T.M.O. 62nd DIVISION.
TMB/2639/H.

Place	Date	Hour	Summary of Events and Information	Remarks and references to Appendices
O.&F.	1st to 3rd.		Nothing to report.	
"	4th.		Trench Mortar Batteries moved to URFT.	
URFT.	5th to 30th.		Nothing to report.	

B.R.Roberts
Captain.R.F.A.
D.T.M.O., 62nd Division.

T2134. Wt. W708—776. 500000. 4/15. Sir J. C. & S.

Original.   Confidential.

War Diary.

Trench Mortar Batteries
Highland Division.

Volume B'27

From. March. 1st. 1919.
To.   March. 31st. 1919.

                        [signature]
                              Captain A.P.A.
                    D.T.M.O. Highland Division
April 3rd. 1919.

Original.

Trench Mortar Bties
Highland Division
Volume 1

WAR DIARY
or
INTELLIGENCE SUMMARY

Army Form C. 2118.

Instructions regarding War Diaries and Intelligence Summaries are contained in F.S. Regs., Part II. and the Staff Manual respectively. Title pages will be prepared in manuscript.

Place	Date	Hour	Summary of Events and Information	Remarks and references to Appendices
URFT	March 1st 1919		Majority of men attached to Field Batteries for duty.	
"	2.3.19 to 31.3.19.		Nothing to report.	

April 2nd 1919.

[signature] Captain RHA.
O.T.M.O. Highland Division

www.ingramcontent.com/pod-product-compliance
Lightning Source LLC
Chambersburg PA
CBHW081449160426
43193CB00013B/2420